*Reheated & Revised*

# The Sauna Is

### by Bernhard Hillila

Illustrations by Nancy Hillila
Graphic design by M. A. Cook
Cover by David Fitzsimmons
Editors: Dwayne M. and Joan Liffring-Zug Bourret,
Dorothy Crum, Maureen Patterson,
Stephanie Schatz, and Melinda Bradnan

*Penfield*
BOOKS

# Acknowledgments

The Finnish Sauna Society, Helsinki, Finland, especially Chairman Professor Harald Teir, M.D., and Pirkko Valtakari, Executive Secretary.

Martin A. Halttunen, for providing technical information regarding sauna heating.

Marshall Harvey, for his comments on the manuscript.

Houghton Mifflin Company, for permission to use some quotations from the book *Laughing Boy* by Oliver LaFarge. Copyright renewed 1957 by Oliver LaFarge.

Herbert Gold, for permission to use a quotation from the article "Sweating It Out Together," published in the September 7, 1975, book review section of the *Los Angeles Times*.


**Books by Mail**
This book, *The Sauna Is,* $11.95, postage $4.95
For a complete list of all titles send $2.00 to:
Penfield Books, 215 Brown Street, Iowa City, Iowa 52245
or see us on the Web at: www.penfieldpress.com

First printing 1979. Revised edition 1988. Expanded edition 2003.
Copyright © 1988 by Bernhard Hillila. All rights reserved. No part of this book may be reproduced in any form without written permission from the author except by a reviewer who may quote brief passages in a review.
Printed in the United States of America.

Library of Congress Control Number: 2003104479
ISBN 1-932043-09-8

# Contents

Dedication . . . . . . . . . . . . . . . . . . . . . . . . . . . . . . 4
About the Author and Contributors . . . . . . . . . . . . . . . . . 5

# The Sauna Is...

A Part of My Heritage. . . . . . . . . . . . . . . . . . . . . . . . . 7
A Bath That's Different. . . . . . . . . . . . . . . . . . . . . . . . 9
A Bathhouse with a History . . . . . . . . . . . . . . . . . . . . 11
A Gift from the Finns . . . . . . . . . . . . . . . . . . . . . . . . 15
A Bath That's Enjoyable . . . . . . . . . . . . . . . . . . . . . . 19
A Means of Rejuvenation . . . . . . . . . . . . . . . . . . . . . 27
A Spot for Relaxation . . . . . . . . . . . . . . . . . . . . . . . . 31
A Setting for Propriety . . . . . . . . . . . . . . . . . . . . . . . 35
An Aid to Grooming . . . . . . . . . . . . . . . . . . . . . . . . 39
A Room for Heating . . . . . . . . . . . . . . . . . . . . . . . . 41
A Project for Do-It-Yourselfers . . . . . . . . . . . . . . . . . . 43
A Variety of Designs . . . . . . . . . . . . . . . . . . . . . . . . 51
A Bridge Between Cultures . . . . . . . . . . . . . . . . . . . . 53
A Heated Competition . . . . . . . . . . . . . . . . . . . . . . 57
Sauna 101 . . . . . . . . . . . . . . . . . . . . . . . . . . . . . . . 60
Postscript . . . . . . . . . . . . . . . . . . . . . . . . . . . . . . . 63

# Dedication

To my son Marty, my nephew Carl, and all other sauna enthusiasts of their generation.

*Bernhard Hillila and granddaughter Maija Nelson, who wrote the story on page 53.*

# About the Author and Contributors

Bernhard Hillila is a sauna enthusiast and expert, a Valparaiso University professor emeritus, a Lutheran pastor, and a former college president and university dean. He has studied saunas in Finland, he has built saunas, he enjoys saunas, and he knows the physical and mental benefits of sauna bathing.

Born in 1919 of Finnish parents in Gwinn, Michigan, he spoke only Finnish until kindergarten. He graduated from Suomi Theological Seminary (now Lutheran School of Theology at Chicago), earned a master's degree in psychology from Case-Western Reserve University, and earned a doctorate in education from Columbia University. He is a published poet and translator.

In earlier years, Hillila had an interesting hobby — walking the slack wire. His slack wire is a quarter-inch steel cable stretched between supporting aluminum pipes. "It's something I learned from my father," he says. "The slack wire looks easy, but it's difficult. Unlike tightroping, the slack wire will keep whipping back and forth. Every muscle of the body is tense. That wire is awfully nervous, and you must recover quickly or end up on your face or back. Believe me, I have the scars to prove it." He is featured on the wire on the back cover of his book *FinnFun*.

Hillila and his wife, Esther, reside in Valparaiso, Indiana. They have three children and three grandchildren. His granddaughter, Maija Nelson, contributed an essay about her sauna experiences in Finland. David Maki, a Houghton, Michigan, writer and assistant editor of the *Finnish American Reporter*, wrote the essay about the Finnish Sauna Heat Contest.

Nancy (Mrs. Martin) Hillila, the daughter-in-law of the author and an art graduate of Wittenberg University, provided illustrations. The cover art was provided by David Fitzsimmons, noted Tucson cartoonist and nephew-in-law of Esther Hillila, wife of the author.

# A Part of My Heritage

The main purpose of this book is to provide reliable information about the sauna. Although the sauna is growing in popularity in the United States and throughout the world, there are many to whom the concept is strange, perhaps frightening. To such readers this volume is an invitation to explore the sauna, to become better acquainted with it, and to enjoy it as a very natural and healthful experience.

In this age of slick promotion, the concept of the sauna has at times been misunderstood and misrepresented. Perhaps this book can help someone unlearn misinformation about the sauna. We need some cold facts about that very hot place. I therefore define the authentic sauna, describe the bathing experience, and consider related historical, physiological, psychological, and moral issues. Information about sauna construction is also provided. It is not my intent to create sauna snobs. A sauna snob is as obnoxious as a wine snob or an art snob.

May this book simply enable more people to experience the joys of an authentic sauna, as other books have helped readers to enjoy a vintage wine or to appreciate a great work of art. Since the mood of the sauna is one of relaxation and shared enjoyment, the style of this work naturally reflects that spirit.

The information presented has come from many sources. First of all, the sauna has been part of my family's lifestyle ever since I can remember; we have usually had a sauna in our home. Fascinated by this aspect of my ethnic heritage, I have read everything I have been able to find concerning the subject in Finnish, English, and German. I researched the subject in Finland, discussing sauna matters with numerous knowledgeable persons.

— *Bernhard Hillila*

# A Bath That's Different

Sauna is a Finnish word, typical of a melodious language full of diphthongs. It is natural for Americans to pronounce it "sawna," to rhyme with flora and fauna, but the word should really have an "ow" sound, as in "How now brown sauna?" In a phonetic language such as Finnish, every letter is sounded, including the "u" in "sauna." The word "sauna" refers both to the Finnish bathhouse and to the bath itself.

The sauna provides a bath in which cleansing is accomplished through both perspiration and washing. The bathhouse can be simple or elaborate, but in any case it must include a room in which the air can be heated. The heating is accomplished by a *kiuas* (pronounced "cue us," as in "cue us in"), which is a heating unit covered with stones. The stones are heated until super hot, and the air temperature rises to ranges usually associated with ovens rather than rooms. The ideal temperature is 175–205° Fahrenheit (80–95° Centigrade). Some enthusiasts send the thermometer as high as 230° F (110° C), but such extremes are not recommended. Other bathers are content to sweat it out at temperatures of 160–170° F (70–77° C). The 175–205° range, however, is generally found to be the best.

The relative humidity of the room is increased by throwing small amounts of water on the *kiuas*. (If a Finn offers a sauna cocktail, it's just water on the rocks!) However, the air remains comparatively dry, because much of the moisture is absorbed by the wooden walls, ceiling, and shelves.

To many, heat of 180–230° F sounds simply frightening. "After all, water boils at 212° F!" So it does. But air doesn't. And people don't. Many a cook has placed an arm into a 450° oven without having had the hand fall off or explode. To be cleansed to the nth degree, one should raise the sauna temperature at least to the 175th degree.

It is somewhat of a misnomer to call the sauna a steam bath, since the amount of moisture is small. The basic difference between a Turkish bath and a sauna is that the air in the former is damp and steamy, while the air in the latter is moderately dry. Since the human body can stand much more dry heat than damp heat, the temperatures in the sauna are much higher than those in the Turkish bath. A temperature of 190° in dry air is not as uncomfortable as a temperature of 120° in water-saturated air. ("It's not the heat, it's the humidity!") The sauna is fairly low in moisture — only 15 to 20 percent. Perhaps vapor bath would be a better term for the sauna than steam bath. The Finnish word for the super hot vapor exuding from the stones is *loyly*, which rhymes with absolutely nothing in English. (For those who are especially interested in languages, let me simply say that "ö" sounds like the "o" in "word," "y" sounds like the German "ü" or French "u," "öy" is a diphthong, and all Finnish words are accented on the first syllable. Take it from there!)

 The fluctuating but relatively low moisture content of the air in a sauna is the unique feature, the Finnish finesse, of the sauna. The Roman bath provides a roomful of hot, dry air; the damp Turkish bath gives a roomful of moisture; the Finnish bath gives dry heat to which a little moisture is added. As the wood absorbs moisture, more moisture is added. The air is not so dry that it injures the lungs, but it is dry enough to permit extremely high temperatures and to promote much perspiration. In this age of antiperspirants, it may seem ironic that the Finns promote a perspirant!

 In addition to perspiration in the heat room, thorough washing is an essential part of the sauna experience. The sauna cleanses through alternate applications of heat and water. The Japanese parboiling done in extremely hot water is cleansing, relaxing, and delightful in its own way. The Finnish procedure, however, surrounds the bather with high, moderately dry heat; then it washes him with cool water. The cycle is repeated, heating and cooling, purifying from the inside, washing the outside. The result is deep cleansing and thorough relaxation.

# A Bathhouse with a History

Bathing for cleanliness, like eating for nourishment, is one of the basics of human life. It is characteristic of man, however, to refine life's basics. Food is not just gobbled to satisfy hunger, but the process of eating is enjoyed as much as the full stomach. Thus, cleansing also has become more than the quick removal of dirt. Attention is given to the joys of bathing. (Otherwise we wouldn't have ads for bath oil beads!) At times the process has become almost ritualistic. Ashley Montagu asks whether bathing includes "a ritual revival of pleasures originally enjoyed in the aquatic environment of the mother's womb, and in the early experiences of bathing during infancy."

Different nations have had their various styles of bathing. Ancient Egyptian palaces already had rooms for bathing, but the earliest examples of well-preserved bathing facilities are from the Greek civilization, from the palaces of Knossos and Phaistos (c. 1700–1400 B.C.) and the palaces of Tiryns (c. 1200 B.C.).

Perspiration bathing existed as early as 500 B.C. in Greece, and by 300 B.C. it had become part of the *gymnasion*, the center for arts and physical training. The perspiration bath gradually became a daily routine for many Greek citizens. The Spartans, particularly, bathed in high, dry heat, followed by a plunge into cold water.

The Romans, however, were the real organizers of both the procedures and the facilities of bath taking. To get the full treatment, the Roman went to the *apodyterium* to undress, to the *elaeothesium* or *unctorium* to be anointed with oil, to the *palaestra* for strenuous exercise, to the *caldarium* for the hot-room treatment, to the *sudatorium* or *laconicum* for steam, to the warm *tepidarium* to be scraped with *strigils*, and to the *frigidarium* for a cold bath. In a private home, such a bath could be provided with a series of small rooms; in a public bath, enormous facilities, such as those of Pompeii, were constructed. In either instance, certain essentials had to be provided: a system of circulating hot air and a system of furnishing hot and cold water to various areas. There were lavish bathing establishments called therms, such as the bath complex of Caracalla in Rome, which measured more than 300 square yards, including a stadium, lecture areas, and reading rooms built of marble and mosaic, elaborately furnished and decorated. That is a hard act for even our most elaborate health clubs to follow! In A.D. 300, Rome had 856 public bathhouses plus fifteen therms.

The destruction of the Roman aqueducts contributed to the closing of Roman baths. Furthermore, with the beginning of the Christian era the church fathers urged that bathing be for cleanliness and health rather than for ostentatious luxury. In fact, cleanliness was not very close to godliness in the estimation of some religious leaders: Saint Jerome rebuked some of his disciples for excessive cleanliness; Saint Benedict felt that frequent bathing should not be permitted; Saint Francis even listed dirtiness as a sign of holiness!

From Rome, highly developed baths spread back to Greece and farther to the east. Contrasted with Spartan emphases on exercise and sudden temperature changes, the Turkish bath provided a place to luxuriate in heat and quiet. The heating procedure was the same as in Roman baths, but the facilities were much simpler. Reaching its peak of development in the fifteenth century, the *hammam* declined in the sixteenth century and has had a revival of interest since the nineteenth century. Massage is an integral part of the Turkish bath.

Throughout Europe, bathhouses had come into bad repute by the fourteenth century because of promiscuity associated with them. Bathhouse construction, therefore, received little attention. The famous bath of Marie Antoinette at Versailles, for example, is quite crudely engineered.

Over the centuries, hot baths have developed in a broad variety of styles in different cultures. We shall briefly consider some of the more interesting examples. The Russian *banya*, with roots in the dim past, illustrates bathing in extremely wet heat. That form of hot bath can properly be called a steam bath. In the Far East, the Japanese developed bathing in outdoor wooden tubs that are filled with exceedingly hot water. The entire family may bathe together. Among the Mayas and Aztecs of Central America, the low stove-heated *temascal* developed and attained widespread use.

Many nations have medicinal baths. The city of Bath in England derives its name from the mineral springs that produce 500,000 gallons of water daily at temperatures of 114° to 120° F. Roman baths existed there already in the first century A.D. The term "spa" comes from Spa, Belgium, which is famous for its mineral baths. Vichy in France, Hot Springs in Arkansas, and French Lick in Indiana are other spots where health is sought by bathing.

At times, bathing has been ritualistic, the outward cleansing signifying inner purification. In Britain, the Knights of the Bath actually had a bath in the early form of initiation. The candidate was given a shave, a haircut, and a bath together with instructions regarding the Order before he was dressed in ritual robes and taken to the chapel for his all-night vigil.

The American Indians used sweat baths, but the approach was that of occasional therapy or special ritual cleansing, rather than weekly bathing. The structure was primitive and *ad hoc:* a small, shallow hole was dug and covered by a low roof; red-hot stones were brought in, and water was dashed on them to form steam; one or two persons would endure the steam for a period and then dash to a stream or snow bank. In a classic novel about the Native Americans, *Laughing Boy* by Oliver LaFarge, Slim Girl and Laughing Boy are married with the proper ceremonies. Slim Girl, who has forgotten some of the Navajo ways because of her stay at the reservation school, is eager to begin weaving, but Laughing Boy insists on the ritual bathing: "No, today before we do anything, we must make ourselves clean, we must make a fresh start."

At the close of the book, Slim Girl dies and Laughing Boy buries her, keeps his prescribed vigil of four days, and concludes it with the ritual purification. LaFarge's description is simple and touching:

"He built his sweat lodge, and since it was hard to get mud out of the frozen ground, covered it with blankets. In the mid-afternoon he put in the hot rock, stripped, and entered. He had made it good and hot; he sat in there chanting as long as he could stand it, then he burst out, rolled in the snow, and dressed hastily. He felt infinitely better. He looked at the sun, low in the west; the fourth day was ended. He felt clear-headed, peaceful, washed. . . ."

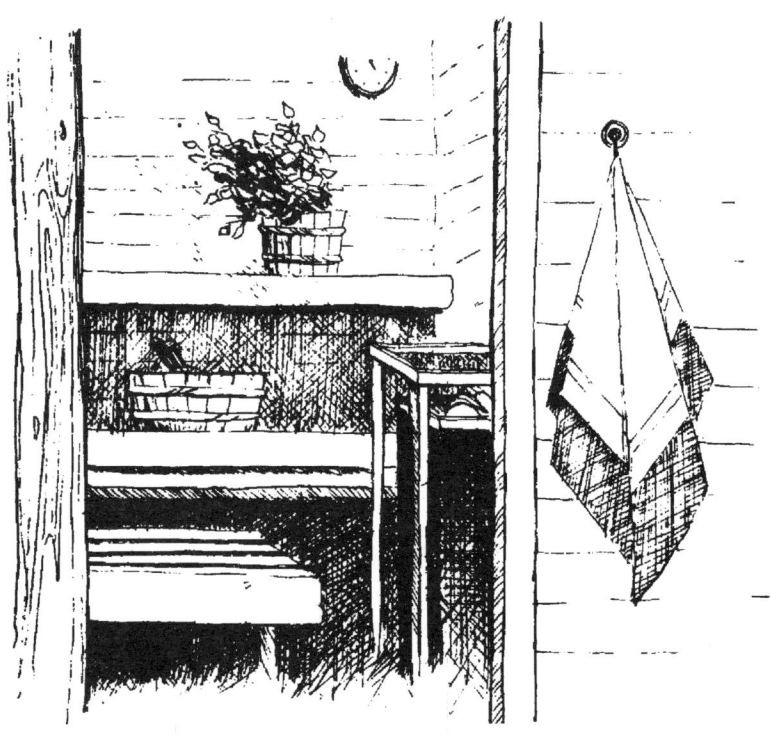

# A Gift from the Finns

From the foregoing brief historical sketch, it is clear that the sauna was prevalent throughout Europe in the Middle Ages. Although it subsequently disappeared from most European countries, the sauna was preserved in Finland and has been reintroduced to the world by that nation. Although not a Finnish invention, it is nevertheless the Finnish development of an ancient European bath culture, and it has acquired a distinctive Finnish character.

Current sauna merchandising often treats the sauna as though it were of generally Scandinavian, rather than specifically Finnish, identity. According to an article in a popular men's magazine, "The great health and beauty secret of Scandinavian men and women is just a lot of hot air. The Scandinavians have been taking saunas for a thousand years and reaping the rewards of health and clear complexions."

Stating the matter more accurately, one must say that the sauna tradition died throughout much of Scandinavia but continued in Finland. To be sure, it recently has been revived throughout Scandinavia and all of Europe, but over the years it is Finland that has been the preserver of sauna culture.

Because of its geographical location, Finland has often been a meeting ground for West and East. Finland joins as well as separates Scandinavia and the Soviet Union. Thus the Finnish form of bathing has developed a synthesis of the Western baths — a pattern coming down from the Middle Ages — and the Eastern steam bathing, which likewise has a long history. The Finnish sauna is a unique combination of the Roman dry heat bath and the Russian wet steam bath.

Reintroduced to the world with a distinctive Finnish character, the sauna is now becoming truly international in its appeal. Finns have taken the sauna wherever they have gone — to Scandinavia, the Soviet Union, Germany, Australia, Canada, and the United States. Finnish colonists brought it to the Delaware Colony in the 1630s, to Alaska in the 1830s, and to Michigan, Minnesota, Ohio, Massachusetts, and other states in the 1880s and 1890s. It is no doubt an apocryphal account that some Finnish immigrants sought employment in "sweat shops," thinking they were saunas! Athletes participating in international Olympics, seamen voyaging to many ports, and emigrants settling in various climates all helped the spread of the sauna. In fact, throughout much of Europe it is rapidly becoming a status symbol of the affluent.

Moreover, the International Sauna Congresses, convened quadrennially by sauna societies of various nations, attract participants from around the world. The sauna thus has truly become a "Finnternational" institution. It is not surprising, in almost any country, to turn a corner and discover a sauna. Transoceanic ships often include saunas. The very word has infiltrated countless languages. A delightful German book is the tiny *Gespräche in der Sauna*. One presumptuous Finn assumed "Finlandization" was the conquest of the world by the Finnish sauna!

Since there are many persons of Finnish extraction in the United States, the sauna has come here, too. It has been estimated that more than 20,000 saunas are being installed annually in the United States.

With the American penchant for merchandising there is, however, a danger that in our land the concept of sauna will be stretched badly out of shape to include sauna belts, sauna facial masks, sauna tubs, sauna cabinets, sauna tents, and steam rooms of all kinds! If the product involves heat, the ad man gets a sudden perspiration and says, "Let's call it sauna! That's an 'in' term." Such "saunas" lose something in the translation. The term "sauna" is properly applied only to baths in which the entire body receives dry heat and steam. It is to be hoped that the rapid spread and increased popularity will not lead to a changed, misdirected pattern. We seek to perpetuate the authentic Finnish bath, to capture the essence of the sauna. Finns by nature are not entrepreneurs, promoters. Perhaps it has been natural for them to allow the sauna to remain the sauna rather than seek new angles for slick merchandising.

In Finland, the bath ritual is not a status symbol to be enjoyed solely by the rich — it is for everyone. To be sure, Carl Gustaf

Mannerheim, Jean Sibelius, and Paavo Nurmi were all sauna enthusiasts, but so is the average citizen.

Currently, about 80 percent of Finland's rural families have their own saunas. There are approximately 800,000 private saunas plus about 400,000 saunas that are public bathhouses or available in hotels, health clubs, hospitals, apartment buildings, and factories. Finland thus has over a million saunas for a population of five million — a sauna for every five persons!

Finland includes 688 miles of coastline, 80,000 coastal islands, 60,000 lakes, and more than 200,000 inland islands; the shores are dotted with saunas. The sauna is the traditional bath of the Finns. It has become an institution, combining cleansing, relaxing, and recreational aspects. The *Encyclopedia Britannica* correctly states that the "Finnish people . . . made [the sauna] a national pastime." However, the inadequate description of bath procedures that follows leaves an impression of the Finnish sauna as a historic rather than current phenomenon. More accurately, it should be said that the sauna in Finland continues to be the national pastime, and elsewhere it is growing in popularity.

For the Finnish farmer, the sauna was versatile in its service. Since it had heat and facilities for cooking and bathing, is was usually the first building built by the homesteader. He lived in the sauna while building his house. After the house was built, the sauna still had many uses besides de-dirting the family: There, meat was cured, flax dried, barley malted, skis waxed, leather worked, and wood shaped for furniture and implements. There, the children were born, the sick treated, the athletes conditioned. The hunter returning from the hunt went to the sauna. The bride preparing for her vows went to the sauna. As a matter of course, the eve of every festival included cleansing in the sauna.

The hygienic values of the sauna gave Finnish troops a plus in the rigors of the Winter War of 1939–40. Field Marshal Carl Gustaf Mannerheim insisted that his soldiers have access to saunas — built on the spot if not available in the area — where the men would be thawed out, refreshed, and cleansed. The Finns expected that they would be attacked by the Russians, but they didn't want to lose to the traditional enemy of all armies: vermin. According to an old Finnish saying, the louse pleads, "Wash me, freeze me, but don't take me into the sauna heat!"

Generally a private sauna is heated once or twice a week. During planting or harvest time, the farm sauna is heated every evening. Typically, the sauna is heated on Saturday evening. The body is thoroughly cleansed, of course, and muscle aches disappear, but the mind is also set at ease, the worries of the job are forgotten, and tensions fade away. Time is given to the family; friends, too, may be invited. In earlier days, when Saturday evening church bells rang in the Sabbath, they put a period to the week's work. That was the time to put away the dirt, the hurry, and the worry of the past week, to relax and bathe, and prepare for the Lord's Day. For the Finn the sauna is still, on any day, a place and time for cleansing, relaxing, and refreshing.

# A Bath That's Enjoyable

Because saunas at present are often found in health clubs and are used in physical fitness, conditioning, and therapy programs, some people have assumed that the sauna experience is primarily a treatment to which one is subjected for remedying some problem, such as being overweight. The definition of "sauna" in *The American Heritage Dictionary of the English Language* reflects that line of thought: "1. A steam-bath treatment originating in Finland, in which the bather is subjected to steam. . . . 2. A room for taking this treatment." That sounds rather grim!

Really, the sauna is intended for enjoyment — and not just by masochistic individuals who enjoy giving themselves pain. It should be a pleasurable experience for all, young and old. The sauna bather should not prepare to be "subjected" to a "treatment," but should plan to give himself a series of enjoyable sensations.

## The Bath Itself

Different people have different patterns of bathing in a sauna. Some stay briefly, others luxuriate for a long time. Some make a single visit to the heat room, others pop in and out many times. Some take moderate heat, throw no water on the rocks for steam, and never touch a whisk; others seem to be masochistic in the intensity of the baking and self-flagellation. There is no rigidly prescribed procedure — one should use the style he enjoys most. Furthermore, an individual may vary his sauna procedure from time to time, depending on the time of day, the congeniality of the company, the condition of his health, and many other factors. A rather typical procedure is outlined here.

First of all, one's clothes should be taken off, of course — all of them. Already in the undressing, one can begin to relax. Hurry should be shed with the clothing. Jewelry and watches should also be removed, because they can become painfully hot to the touch.

A very common procedure is as follows: the bather goes into the heat room for about 15 minutes, taking dry heat to induce perspiration; he then steps under the shower and goes to the dressing room for perhaps 10 minutes of cooling; then there is a second visit to the heat room, making steam and using birch whisks to lightly beat the body; then there is another quick shower, followed by a cooling; there follows a third visit to the heat room for a last, deep roasting; finally there is a thorough soap-and-water washing with brushes and sponges and rinsing with plenty of water. Such a procedure, taking an hour or so in all, is a recurring cycle of heating and cooling. This is the sauna rhythm.

In the heating room, the bathers sit or lie on a series of shelves, like bleachers. Since the heat varies considerably from floor to ceiling, a bather can move higher or lower for maximum enjoyment. The heat in a seven-foot-high sauna can vary from 100° at floor level to 240° at ceiling height, and a seated bather can experience a variation of temperature from 130° F at his toes to 210° F at his head. Lying prone will enable the entire body to receive a uniform heat level. Some saunas have a small wooden rod above the top shelf, so that the feet can be lifted higher for more intense heat. Throwing water on the rocks produces steam and sets strong convection currents in motion from the *kiuas*. The more directly one is in line with the vapor current, the stronger the impact of the heat.

One should be free to leave the steam room whenever he feels he has had enough. Sauna-taking should never be an endurance contest or test of manliness. The aim is not to simulate the pains of purgatory or the pangs of hell, but rather to produce a feeling of well-being. If the air seems painful to breathe upon first entering the heat room, a cool, wet washcloth held over the nose will help.

The acme of the sauna experience is achieved when the shower is replaced by a dip into a lake and when one can sit outside in the altogether, dried by unpolluted breezes. Some brave souls enjoy a roll in the snow or a dip into a hole in an ice-covered lake. While contemplating such an experience can be a shock, the sensation itself is delightful. Some newer hotels in Helsinki provide this breed of enthusiasts a polar-bear opportunity — a tub of 41° water as a change of pace from the heat of the sauna. As steel is tempered by being plunged red-hot into cold water, so the Finnish *sisu* (intestinal fortitude) is supposedly strengthened by this Spartan regimen. Accepting the widely held thesis that man has two systems for temperature sensitivity — one for heat, one for cold — why not give both a workout?

In a charming article entitled "The Sauna Experience: Discover How Life Can Be Beautiful at 200° F.," published in the February 1971 issue of *American Home*, Denise McCluggage describes the snow-rolling experience:

"If it is snowing, I walk out into the night of the deserted countryside and the flakes fall like a constant shower of tiny needles on my lifted arms. The body is so stoked by the heat from the sauna that it steams in the cold air and melts deep molds of itself in the snowbank I drop into. Sweeping my arms at my sides, I imprint an angel shape, laughing to see the snow crystals dissolve on this griddle surface that is me. The feet feel the cold first, leaving incongruous, bare prints to freeze (and baffle the deliveryman the next day). They pad me quickly and dripping back to the womb of the sauna. Water melted from the sky and water brought forth from the body mingle now in a mix of hot and cold with no clear idea of which is which. It's like dry ice. There's a tingle and a glow and it feels just plain fantastic."

After a snow roll, a final trip is made to the steam room to warm up. Some bathers like to take a little heat even after the final showering.

The final drying is a matter of preference: some like a brisk rub with a coarse towel; others prefer a gentle blotting or a simple air drying. In any case, the final cooling, like the rest of the sauna experience, should be unhurried. A restful massage can be included as an additional treat. While in the heat room, what else should one do? Just relax and not think of additional activity. The comment of one of my friends is typical of our high-pressure age:

"It seems such a waste of time. If I could read something, I'd feel it would be more worthwhile." Part of the benefit of the sauna, however, lies in the very fact that one sets aside a time for relaxation pure and simple. To be sure, I have recently seen advertisements for a particular brand of prefabricated sauna showing a young couple perusing a magazine. That, however, is not in the spirit of the Finnish sauna. Reading would be impractical in any case: the lighting is not designed to be reading light; one's reading glasses would become foggy; and the binding of a favorite volume would become unglued!

Beyond the impracticality, there is the weightier consideration of the spirit of the sauna. In the sauna one doesn't ask for additional ways to while away the time but focuses on the sensory experiences of the bath itself. In the sauna one doesn't strive for intellectual stimulation but rather for mental relaxation and pleasing sensation.

The whisk has been mentioned several times. This *vihta*, as the Finns name it (or *vasta* in eastern Finland) is preferably made of young white birch, although cedar (arbor vitae), oak, or even eucalyptus can be used. Leafy twigs about a foot and a half to two feet long are tied into bundles of a dozen to two dozen. (If the whisks are to be frozen for future use, they are usually made a bit smaller to conserve space in the freezer.) The twigs should be cut from medium-sized trees to ensure full, green leaves, yet supple branches. The branches should be free of catkins, which can easily fall off during vigorous whisking.

In Finland, the traditional time for *vihta* making is the week following Mid-summer's Day, June 24. In a warmer climate, such as in Ohio, for example, the optimal time is generally a month earlier. The *vihta* can be dried by hanging it in a dry, warm spot. It can then be prepared for use by soaking it in warm water as the sauna is heating. The properly made *vihta* is remarkably durable, remaining green, pliable, and aromatic, reusable for an entire year. To be assured of the authentic verdant breath of summer in the bleak midwinter, however, it is best to make a number of whisks and to slip some into the freezer, so that a fresh one may be taken at any time. One can simply slip a whisk into a plastic bag, add a little salt to preserve color, and slip it into the freezer next to the broccoli and strawberries! It can be thawed out at room temperature whenever needed.

The whisks are used to gently slap the skin, beginning with the neck and ending with the soles of the feet. Besides setting the hot air in motion to further stimulate perspiration, the whisking stimulates circulation in the capillaries, provides soothing massages for muscles, and tones the skin. The birch twigs also give the sauna a delightful fragrance.

The sauna is to smell only of clean air, sweet wood, and birch leaves. The heat room should be properly ventilated; perspiration is to be felt, not smelled!

Even small children are taught that the sauna is a place to go for a bath; it is not a place to go to the bathroom. Food and drink should be enjoyed in the dressing room or dining area, not in the heat room. Pouring port or sherry instead of water on the *kiuas* is a waste of good wine and an insult to the sauna.

Many persons find it particularly enjoyable to combine exercise and sauna bathing. A good workout in tennis, swimming, bowling, or jogging, followed by relaxing and cleansing heat, is a most satisfying experience.

The following guidelines, based on recommendations of the Finnish Sauna Society (*Sauna-Seura* r.y.), provide a good guide to sensible sauna bathing:

"Allow yourself a reasonable amount of time. Have a shower before entering the heat room. Use a cover on the bench, for hygienic reasons. The temperature in the sauna should be 80–100° C (176–212° F). Increase the humidity by throwing water on the stones.

"Refresh yourself after the first heating by showering, cooling out of doors, or swimming. You may now go to the heat room a second time and whisk yourself with the birch twigs. It is unwise and unhealthful to compete with others in tolerating high temperatures. You can alternate the heating and the cooling as many times as you wish. Have another session in the heat room before washing. Finally, refresh with a shower and a brisk rub. People suffering from heart complaints or from high blood pressure should avoid rapid cooling after having had a sauna. Dress only after you have cooled to normal body temperature.

"Think of your health: big meals and alcohol should be avoided before the sauna. Think also of the other sauna users: leave the sauna clean, tidy, and ventilated — as you would expect to find it."

The following "Sauna Beatitudes" also give some indication of the behavior and spirit which should prevail in a sauna.

## Sauna Beatitudes

Blessed are those who shower before sitting on the shelves; they deserve the best seats.

Blessed are the considerate, who ask their sauna mates whether they want more steam; they are valued as sauna partners.

Blessed are those who bathe quietly and pleasantly, for the sauna is a place of peace.

Blessed are those who do their switching at a comfortable distance from others, for they make the bath a pleasure for all.

Blessed are the pure in heart, for they shall see nothing dirty in an unclothed body.

Blessed are those who wash others' backs, for they shall receive back washings.

Blessed are those who leave the sauna clean; they are welcome in any sauna.

## Sauna Hospitality

In our culture, people often invite friends into the home for a meal, for coffee, or for cocktails. Even one's best friends, however, might wince if they were invited to come for a bath; they might think someone is trying to tell them something! In Finland, however, it is very natural to ask friends or neighbors to come for sauna. As more Americans build saunas, this custom will develop naturally.

For overnight guests who may have traveled far, what greater hospitality can be offered than a relaxing and cleansing sauna, followed by something to eat, good fellowship, and a sound sleep?

After a sauna, one is thirsty and hungry. Beer, soft drinks, or fruit juices may be served while the bathers are cooling and drying in the dressing area. After all have bathed, something more may be offered — coffee and sandwiches, beer and pizza, or a supper. Since much salt is lost through perspiration, something salty hits the spot and fills a physiological need. There are some who like to cook their supper while they are roasting themselves, and so they put foil-wrapped sausage on the *kiuas* and eggs straight from the refrigerator on the top bathing shelf. When they are through with their baths, the sausage and eggs are ready to be eaten with bread and beverage! However, the heat room of a sauna is not really a food-preparation area, nor is the *kiuas* intended to be a hotdog grill. The sights and smells and residue of cooking distract from the bath itself. It is better to have the cooking done in the kitchen or with a small unit in the dressing area.

One should not offer a sauna soon after a meal. The blood which is needed for digestive processes should not be sidetracked to skin capillaries. If time is limited, the sauna should come first, the meal afterward. Bathe now, eat later. If a big meal is served, the diners should wait at least an hour before taking a sauna.

The sauna host is concerned about hospitality for his guest. The other side of the coin is considerate behavior by the bathers. The bather should leave the sauna clean for the next user; he should take switches, wet washcloths, and used shelf cloths out of the heat room and rinse the platform with a bucketful of clean water; in the washroom, he should clean and hang up brushes, sponges, luffas, and washcloths; he should not leave the dressing room strewn with wet towels, hair nets, bottles, and caps.

The considerate host will make it easy for sauna guests to be tidy by providing hooks for clothes, shelves for beauty aids, and waste baskets for discards. He also will care for his sauna after each use: rinsing the shelves and floor of the heat room, leaning the duckboards (removable floor boards) up against the wall, and thoroughly ventilating the heat room and washing area until dry. He will regularly scrub the shelves and floors.

# A Means of Rejuvenation

Physiologically, many things happen in the sauna: perspiration begins, skin temperature rises, the heartbeat quickens, blood circulation accelerates, the entire body reacts to the stimulus of very high heat. Muscles, blood vessels, nerves, and glands have special responses. The skin becomes ruddy. (That no doubt has given the inspiration for the comment: "You're blushing like the backside of a sauna bather!")

Normally, skin temperature is considerably lower than body temperature. In the heat of the sauna, however, skin temperature soon becomes higher than body temperature. As the Finns say, "It's fun and so hot that your navel will smoke!" The blood begins to circulate more rapidly, the sweat glands begin to work, and the pores pour. The wet skin results not from condensation of steam, as in a Turkish (wet steam) bath, but rather from perspiration. Perspiring makes the skin less sensitive to the intense heat. Wetting the skin before entering the heat room also helps. Generally, evaporation of liquid from the skin surface cools the body. In the sauna, however, heat is supplied faster than it is lost. Therefore, body temperature rises in the sauna by as much as three degrees. Further changes are triggered — in chemical reactions, in metabolism, in quickening blood circulation. In the sauna, the heartbeat may be increased from 100 to 160, and twice as much blood may be pumped per minute as during normal rest. The metabolism rate is increased 20 percent. As athletes trying to meet prescribed weight limits well know, even three pounds of weight can be lost by intense use of the sauna.

Are all these physiological changes good or bad? First of all, there is, no doubt, the plus of thorough cleanliness. Some cleansing, like some beauty, is only skin deep. In the Finnish sudatory rite of purification, one becomes clean from the inside out. As Kermit Holt, travel editor of the *Chicago Tribune*, expresses it, "Compared with you, Mr. Clean on the TV commercials is a dirty old man." For that "cleansing" feeling, there is nothing like a thermal bath.

Built for good health and hygiene, bathhouses nevertheless have been accused at times of spreading disease. It is true, of course, that public bathhouses particularly may spread athlete's foot and other diseases if they are not kept meticulously clean. The sauna, however, is a very sanitary place if properly operated: each bather sits on his own towel while bathing, the steam and shower rooms are cleaned after each use, and the high temperature sanitizes.

Furthermore, there is the benefit of extending the range of body responses. Contrasted with a generally moderate, tepid environment, the extreme of the thermal bath can be healthfully stimulating. After a sauna, all systems are "go." In a paper read at the Sixth International Sauna Congress in 1974, Professor Antti Eisalo states:

"The most prominent cardiovascular change during a sauna bath is an increase in the pulse rate and cardiac output . . . In the sauna, the body protects itself against the hot environmental atmosphere to preserve the body temperature. Circulation increases, resulting in heat loss through radiation, conduction, convection — sweating becomes more efficient. These adjustments to secure heat loss resemble those in physical exercise . . . The circulatory variables during the sauna bath are numerically close to the ones measured in jogging. Jogging is popular nowadays, and the sauna could easily be accepted as a substitute by those not interested in jogging . . ."

The challenge of the sauna to body processes is not dangerous. A person's at-rest metabolism rate is increased 20 percent by a sauna but as much as 400 percent by a strenuous walk!

The sauna is not an effective weight reducer. The weight loss is almost entirely water, which is soon replaced. The skin and muscle tone are improved, however, and that is an important consideration for everyone, especially for the weight-watcher.

For some conditions, the sauna can be particularly helpful. Since the bathing facility is antiseptic due to high heat, communicable diseases can be checked more easily. The high heat and gentle whisking provide relief for itching mosquito bites. Skin diseases, muscular aches, and rheumatism generally are helped by saunas. Three old sayings express the Finns' confidence in the health-giving qualities of the sauna: "The sauna is Finland's medicine"; "The sauna is a poor man's pharmacy"; and "If sauna, whisky, and tar won't help, that's the end."

Besides the health benefits derived directly from the sauna, use of the sauna often encourages exercise or massage, which further contribute to well-being.

Like any good thing, the sauna can be abused. The bathers should take steam for pleasure, not to test each other's endurance. The sauna is not a trial-by-fire test of manhood. One of our sauna mugs bears the inscription, *"Hullu kylöpöö, jotta nahka pallaa,"* which may be translated, "It's a madman that bathes until his skin is scorched."

Persons with any dangerous health problems should be careful regarding any test to their systems. Individuals with advanced pulmonary tuberculosis, heart disease, acute inflammation of eyes or nasal passages, or chronic nose bleeding should avoid saunas. Babies, pregnant women, or persons on strong medication should be cautious about saunas. Generally, however, saunas are not dangerous places. In Finland, one-year-olds, invalids, and octogenarians alike thrive on the sauna. According to the law of averages, of course, some people may become ill in a sauna. After all, actress Maria Montez died in a hot tub bath!

In the sauna a very unusual combination of processes develops: a person sits peacefully at rest while his blood vessels, nerves, and glands work hard. After such an experience, the person may well feel that he has had a strenuous workout, even though he has been quite relaxed and at ease. It is difficult to gain a greater sense of physical renewal than that which is provided by this unique combination of exertion and rest.

Any healthful procedure can become a cure-all for its overzealous advocates: the importance of good nutrition can become food faddism; the benefits of sunshine can lead to dry, parched, or even damaged skin; and the thermal bath can become a panacea for the hydropathists or "bath quacks." One can, however, be an enthusiastic supporter of the sauna, using it for thorough cleanliness, physiological conditioning, and relaxation, without becoming a "sauna freak" who expects magical healing effects for everything from flat feet to weak eyesight.

Since 1937, the Sauna Society of Finland has gathered information and encouraged research regarding the sauna. It has been established that, by 1987, more than one thousand works had been published dealing with various aspects of the sauna. Most interest has been focused on medical and physiological effects of the sauna. A number of doctoral dissertations have been written on the sauna. Concerned about the health-related issues involved, scientists, especially in the past two decades, have developed a surprisingly large number of research studies regarding the physiological effects of the sauna. Findings of these studies are regularly reported and discussed at the quadrennial meetings of the International Sauna Congress and subsequently published for broader dissemination.

# A Spot for Relaxation

The sauna-goer seeks psychotherapy as well as physiotherapy from his sauna. If he were inclined toward bilingual punning, he would say he strives for *mens sana in corpore sauna*. One of the basic differences between the shower and the sauna is that one can rush the former but not the latter. The sauna was not built for saving time but for spending it well — for having a precious interval in which one just sits, doesn't see anyone dashing, isn't bombarded by sounds, adds nothing to the gross national product. (In fact, he reduces the national gross a bit!) The sauna is not something to pop into for ten minutes after handball before dashing to a meeting. A clock in a sauna is truly an anachronism.

I remember having sauna at what is perhaps the finest sauna in the world — the Sauna Society establishment outside of Helsinki. I had asked for a scrubber after my steam, so I took the tag with my number to the lady on duty. She said, "Fine! I'm going for coffee now, and I'll scrub you after a while."

I suppose there was something in my expression which conveyed, "I'm ready to be scrubbed right now," because she said, "You're not in a hurry, of course, if you're taking a sauna." Touché.

The sauna is a place to relax. It's a drugless tranquilizer. Cares and tensions seem to dissolve in the heat. Resentment melts away. A Finnish couplet expresses it well:

> *"Saunassa viha viilenee,*
> *Saunassa sammuu sappi."*

A free translation conveys the thought:

> "Anger cools in the sauna,
> Resentment fades away."

One seems to let off steam figuratively as he takes steam literally.

Somehow, superheated air is not an atmosphere conducive to heated arguments. For that reason, many disagreements have been resolved in the sauna. Lin Yutang recommended taking one's adversary to dinner to talk through a difference of opinion; the Finn recommends taking him to sauna. Perhaps the setting is conducive to honesty and to getting at the bare facts of an issue; rank and status disappear with the clothing, and one must communicate simply as one imperfect individual who must accept another individual, warts and all. If Henry Kissinger could have put the Vietnam adversaries into a sauna, much sweat would have been required but less blood and fewer tears. Seriously, not even De Gaulle could have looked pompous in a steam bath!

The most widely known sauna in Helsinki is that of the President at Tamminiemi. The heat room can accommodate as many as eight bathers. Prominent leaders of Finland and of other nations have taken steam in that sauna. Perhaps part of the answer to the riddle of former President Urho K. Kekkonen's success in dealing with both East and West is to be found in his use of sauna consultations! In welcoming the Sixth International Sauna Congress to Helsinki in 1974, President Kekkonen said of the sauna: "It is a great leveler: there are no ministers, VIP's, laborers, or lumberjacks on the sauna platform, only sauna mates. For me — as for most other Finns — the sauna is a way of life. In its heat I forget the workaday stress and can meet my friends and acquaintances."

Possibly the sauna strategy has also aided the government of Finland in its basic deliberations. It has been the custom of the Finnish cabinet to gather at 4 p.m. on Wednesday at Kesäranta, the official residence of the Prime Minister. The first item on the agenda is the sauna. After an hour and a half of steam cleaning, the cabinet members move on to formal deliberations. The parboiled officials are perhaps a little less brittle after the bath. Even inflation doesn't seem as ominous after one has endured 200° of heat. Kesäranta is also the locale for other important governmental and diplomatic meetings. The sauna is generally a prelude to the official business.

The Finnish government also has a large sauna at the Konigstedt estate. Some cabinet member usually is host at a weekly sauna for governmental leaders. Members of the Finnish Parliament, too, have access to a sauna and pool at Santahamina Military Academy.

For persons in diverse walks of life, involved perhaps in

conferences or in a period of worry and pressure, the sauna may be just what the doctor should order. The sauna is a natural place for students to unwind after examinations. There the tension-ridden businessman can shed stress along with his clothes; there the harried homemaker can wash away her worries as well as dirt; there even the care-burdened cleric can better remember that the Church is in God's hands.

The late Finnish Bishop Eino Sormunen is reputed to have remarked after a sauna at the parsonage in Juva: "Only after taking a sauna does there come a time when I can think calmly about our church headquarters in Helsinki."

After the sauna, one feels relaxed. Clair M. Hekhuis, a Dutch friend who is related to the sauna through marriage, wrote one of his newspaper columns about the sauna. He said that the sauna made a person "relaxed as a wet noodle." That says it well. After a sauna one doesn't worry about insomnia, and one doesn't need a prescription for a tranquilizer!

In a *Los Angeles Times* piece entitled "Sweating It Out Together," Herbert Gold describes the delights of sauna as he experienced them in Finland:

"Sauna gives a quasi-religious sense of communion with both history and the present, with friends, memories, and one's own preoccupying body. Yes, we had sauna with hickory logs, panfuls of water on the stove, scalding steam, and then that plunge into an icy lake; yes, it was good, good, good — one felt so clean and verbless."

In this age of artifice and camouflage, the sauna is one of the last bastions of honesty. Did the ancients not say, *"In sudore veritas"* ("In sweat there is truth")? Thousands of ads make us fearful that we're not adequate if we lack the proper mascara or hair spray or girdle; that our image is poor if we don't have the proper aftershave and sports car. In the sauna, however, "just as I am, without one stitch," without any cover-up or improvement, one still is a person — truly more so than with all that other stuff. In the heat room, the man whose chest and stomach are in inverse proportions accepts himself. What is more, his fellow bathers accept him; he doesn't have to take a Charles Atlas course to be fully human. Here is basic honesty: there is nothing "put on" about the sauna bather.

Currently there is much interest in developing man's sensory awareness more fully. Books are written on touching. Montessori and other educational approaches seek to develop tactile sensitivity, and groups at Esalen and elsewhere try to develop greater awareness to all sensory stimuli. The sauna is helpful in developing tactile and kinesthetic sensitivity. Most of all, one *feels* the sauna experience: the lighting is dim, restful; the sounds are unobtrusive; avenues of sensation which are often neglected now become prominent. The entire human envelope feels the heat; skin and muscles are sensitized with birch whisks; there is awareness to sensations in nasal passages, lungs, heart, eyes, toenails, muscles, and joints. A person can appreciate the intricate and responsive physiological equipment with which he is endowed.

In addition to giving a person greater physical self-awareness, the sauna enables a person to reach out and touch another human being. Sauna etiquette requires the bather to offer to wash his partner's back. If one scrubs his neighbor's back, the distance is bridged somewhat; he has reached out and touched his neighbor more helpfully than merely by shaking a hand.

The importance of the skin in sense experience has been underscored recently. One of the most stimulating works on the subject is *Touching: The Human Significance of the Skin*, by Ashley Montagu. According to Montagu:

". . . Physiologically the skin has four functions: (1) as a protector of underlying parts . . .; (2) as a sense organ; (3) as a temperature regulator; and (4) as a metabolic organ in the metabolism and storage of fat, and in water and salt metabolism by perspiration."

The skin — the largest, most sensitive, and most important of our sense organs — should not be taken for granted or abused; it should be cared for and appropriately stimulated. The sauna can be a place for sensitizing the sensors, resetting the body's thermostat, and gently prodding the processes of metabolism. The sauna is an adventure in physiological awareness.

# A Setting for Propriety

The authentic Finnish sauna is certainly no threat to morals. In public saunas, men and women bathe in separate areas or on different days of the week. In private saunas, mixed bathing generally is done only within a family. While a sauna bath by definition should be a sensual experience, it doesn't follow that it should be a sexual one.

There are nevertheless natural reasons why some people find it difficult to associate the sauna with clean minds as well as with clean bodies. For some people, nudity of any sort, even in sleeping, has sexy connotations. Any necessary nakedness, as in bathing, should, in their opinion, be in complete privacy within one's own bathroom or shower stall. They fear that nude bathing, even with members of the same sex, leads to heightened erotic interest.

In the sauna, however, nudity is not the objective; it is merely a necessary condition for bathing properly. Supporters of the sauna are not nudists — they believe in wearing clothes before and after sauna. Perhaps the sauna can aid all of us who have begun life unclothed to maintain a natural acceptance of nakedness in its proper place. In the heat bath, clothes should be our only hang-ups!

Further reason for suspicion about the morality of saunas is the knowledge that, in the past, immorality has, in fact, invaded bathhouses of many types. Thus, a *bagnio* is either a bathhouse or a brothel — the relationship is clear. "Stew" likewise refers to either kind of "house." The abuse of baths has usually developed when mixed bathing has been in style in a permissive society.

There has undeniably been mixed bathing in sauna-type baths in many lands and in many periods throughout history. The response of different peoples has run the gamut from gross licentiousness to virtuous restraint. In some instances, the mixed bathing sank to immorality because the setting was used for sexual excitement; in other instances, the mixed bath was a tribute to morality because the participants took basically a natural, almost asexual approach to it. In no situation is the Chinese proverb more applicable: "In looking at anything, what is behind the eyes is at least as important as what is in front of the eyes." The mind surely is the primary human sex organ.

There are clearly documented times of immorality in public baths. During the heyday of the Roman Empire, bathing became a dallying pastime of the rich; lovers and courtesans were included in the carousing which went on in the bathhouses, as Ovid and Juvenal indicate in their writings. Strict laws regulating the use of public baths were enacted in the times of Hadrian and Justinian, but Heliogabalus and Caligula were very permissive. In Europe, from the late thirteenth century to the early sixteenth century, mixed sauna bathing was common and in many cases was associated with partying and immorality. That pattern, no doubt, led to the decline of the sauna throughout much of Europe in the sixteenth century.

There are also many examples of mixed bathing in which the morals were as clean as the bodies. The Aztecs of Mexico and the Mayas of Guatemala seem to have enjoyed the heat baths in respectable fashion. The baths of Bath, England, the *banyas* of Russia, and the saunas of Finland have mostly been successful in keeping even mixed baths morally sound.

Because the sauna has at times been corrupted, legislation has often forbidden mixed bathing and has stipulated either separate saunas for men and women or has specified separate bathing days for the two sexes. At other times, saunas have been outlawed altogether. Laws at some periods allowed the mixing of sexes as long as the social classes — the nobility and the commoners — were kept separate. At still other times, bathing could be sexually but not racially mixed. Some of the most interesting restrictions on mixed bathing come from the pronouncements of the Orthodox Church Council convened in the middle of the sixteenth century by Ivan the Terrible: mixed bathing by husband and wife as well as between monks and nuns was prohibited!

The Finn has had a reverent attitude toward the sauna. Two old Finnish sayings illustrate that attitude:

"Two places are holy — church and sauna."

"In the sauna one should behave as in church."

After all, the Finns believe cleanliness is next to godliness. In the sauna one should sit peacefully and behave decorously. Loud talk, profanity, dirty stories, and singing are discouraged; jostling and "horsing around" are frowned upon. The nudity of the sauna bathers is a requisite for thorough cleansing, not an end in itself, as for the exhibitionist or voyeur. Denise McCluggage states it well in an article entitled: "The Sauna Experience: Discover How Life Can Be Beautiful at 200° F." (*American Home*, February 1971):

"It may well be that the Finns' reverent attitude toward the sauna has preserved it as an institution whereas other great bath cultures, such as the Romans', floundered and died in debauchery and disease. Without ritualization, the Japanese tea ceremony would be nothing more than a tea bag swished around in hot water . . . . And without its spirit, the sauna would slip into seedy disrepute."

The Finnish sauna, therefore, is not designed as a setting for promiscuity. It really isn't as sexy as a shower or tub bath. After all, there are more comfortable environments for love-making than wooden shelves in 190° heat! If taking a cold shower is effective in removing passion, an hour of baking plus cold showering should be even more of a cure. Thus those modern sauna ads which picture young couples in sexy poses are suggesting something different from the traditional sauna experience. For the Finns the vapor bath has been basically an adjunct of the home. It is a facility to which friends are invited, to be sure, but usually the bathing is one family at a time or the men and women separately.

There are, undeniably, persons in Finland as well as other lands who participate in mixed sauna bathing. In television coverage of the 1976 Winter Olympics at Innsbruck, Austria, Pierre Salinger gave the world-wide viewing audience a peek at such a mixed sauna group. After all, mixed skinny dipping, nudist colonies, and other uninhibited nude activities by both sexes have their adherents in various lands.

The basic thrust of the Finnish sauna, however, is clearly on the side of moral propriety and good manners. We currently live in a permissive age, when some people are tempted to misuse the sauna and bring it into disrepute again. From time to time one reads about a "sauna" operation being used as a cover for prostitution. Such sauna-and-sin promoters prostitute not only the girls but also the concept of sauna. The unadulterated Finnish sauna isn't that kind of hot spot. To make of the cleanest possible place something sleazy, tawdry, pornographic is unforgivable.

In the natural setting of the home, of course, the sauna is considered an aid to marital intimacy. A man and woman who are thoroughly cleansed, freed of tension and hurry, and who possess heightened sensory awareness are best able to find intimacy natural and pleasing.

Many persons use a sauna as a hangover cure, to steam out the aftereffects of a spree. A vapor bath may help alleviate that kind of sickness as well as many others. However, the sauna itself is not a place for boozing. Sauna and alcohol don't mix well. Since overindulging in food, drink, or sauna is hurtful, putting all those evils together could be lethal. The sauna is for persons in possession of their faculties, sensitive to the pleasures of sense; it is not for those who are on some artificial high or low, with numbed reflexes. Only the *kiuas* should be stoned. The sauna is a place for whisks, not whiskey. Some Finns are vigorous in their drinking and rigorous in their bathing, but the two should not be combined.

# An Aid to Grooming

Some members of the fairer sex hesitate to indulge in a sauna because of hair problems. Hair should be a woman's crowning glory — does the sauna make it just a tangle of seaweed? The problem is not insurmountable. After all, did you ever see a mermaid who didn't have beautiful hair? In *South Pacific*, Mary Martin looked great during and after a hair-washing. Having a sauna isn't really such a hair-raising experience. Nevertheless, a complex coiffure may present some problems. There are several procedures which may help a woman to cope with the situation.

First of all, hair-washing should be part of the sauna procedure. Even if the hair is covered by a shower cap or towel in the heat room, the scalp will perspire, and the hair will need washing. Bathing weekly in sauna is, in fact, an excellent first step for good scalp care, which contributes to healthy hair.

Some ladies use the sauna for special hair treatment, rubbing oil into the scalp and covering the hair before stepping into the heat room. There the oil is warmed and absorbed by the hair, leaving a luster after the shampoo. The oil chosen should not have an overpowering odor which will permeate the sauna.

After shampooing, some sauna addicts put their hair up in curlers and go back to the heat room to let it dry rapidly. The more common procedure these days is to use an electric dryer in the dressing room. There are also those who like a late evening bath, followed by a sound sleep and a turbaned trip to the hairdresser as the first thing — well, almost the first thing — in the morning.

If a woman hesitates to be seen without each lash mascaraed, each tinted wave in place, perhaps she will feel uncomfortable at a casual coffee hour or supper following the bath. The sauna, like the swimming pool and strenuous sports, encourages the natural look. After a sauna, beauty is at least skin deep. The sauna does give the skin an aura, and it is said that a woman looks her most beautiful an hour after sauna. What a way to glow! Perspiration bathing is more effective than surface scrubbing, both for removing dead outer skin and for cleansing pores. In the sauna, perspiration is the name of the game; dead skin is removed, and live skin is rejuvenated. The skin surely is clean after a sauna.

Deep-cleansed by perspiration and surface-cleansed by water, soap, and washcloth, the complexion is generally improved. Acne sufferers are helped, and psoriasis itching is usually relieved. All bathing removes natural oils from the skin, causing it to dry somewhat; therefore, a skin cream or moisturizing lotion applied after cooling is beneficial, since it will replenish natural oils. Fingernails and toenails are at their most pliable after the heat, vapor, and water of the sauna have done their work. Thus, for many, the best time for manicuring and pedicuring is shortly after the heat bath.

# A Room for Heating

In this energy-conscious age, consideration must be given to the amount and type of energy used by the sauna. If buildings should be heated at most to 70° or so, is it legitimate to heat any room, even a little wee one, just once a week, to 180°?

Anyone planning installation of a sauna should consider the options available for heating and should choose the fuel that is most energy efficient and yet practical for the particular situation. The three basic fuel options are wood, gas, and electricity.

Just as there is a boom currently in the use of wood stoves for home heating, so there is also a resurgence of interest in wood-fired sauna heaters. Wood was, of course, the original fuel for heating saunas, and it continues to be the most natural. Wood-fired units require a flue to a chimney, but the installation is generally quite simple. This option does require the sauna owner to attend to his sauna heating, rather than relying on a switch to do the work; he must lay in an adequate supply of firewood, carry the wood to the burner, keep the fire burning well, and eventually take out the ashes. Those, however, are tasks which, in their old-fashioned simplicity, many people find enjoyable and relaxing. (Ask any fireplace enthusiast.) There is an old saying, "He who cuts his own firewood warms himself twice." He who cuts his own sauna wood gives himself a double workout for physical conditioning.

Gas-fired sauna units must be properly vented when installed, but such venting usually can be accomplished quite simply. A gas heater can heat a 5'x6'x7' sauna (comfortable for two persons) to 180° F by burning 25 cubic feet of gas. The cost will naturally vary with changes in charges by the supplier, with the size of room heated, and with the temperature desired.

Even though electricity is generally the most costly option to operate, it may be the most practical choice for many. Since no flues or vents are required, installation is simple and moderate in cost. The cost of operating an electric sauna heater is quite reasonable, contrary to the expectations of many.

Cost will vary, of course, according to electric rates and size of unit. Home sauna heaters may draw as little as two kilowatts (for a one-person sauna) or as much as eight kilowatts (for a four-person sauna) or even more for still larger installations. The wattages of heaters appropriate for different sizes of saunas are readily available from dealers. A typical two-person sauna draws approximately the same electricity as a clothes dryer.

From the foregoing, it is obvious that, throughout most of the United States, the cost of weekly heating of a modest-sized sauna is surprisingly low. The heating units are remarkably efficient, the heated rocks retain heat for a long time, and the prescribed wall and ceiling insulation prevents heat loss. A prospective sauna owner should, of course, acquire the most energy-efficient option he can and operate it without waste.

Below are some specifications for wood, gas, and electrical heating units recommended for various sizes of heating rooms.

| Heat Room Dimensions | Room Volume (cubic feet) | Number of Bathers | Wood Stove Fire Box (cubic feet) | Gas Heater (BTUs) | Electric Heater (BTUs) |
|---|---|---|---|---|---|
| 4'x4'x7' | 112 | 1 | 2.5 | 7,500 | 2.2 |
| 4'x6'x7' | 168 | 2 | 3.0 | 11,000 | 3 |
| 5'x6'x7' | 210 | 2 | 4.0 | 13,750 | 4 |
| 6'x6'x7' | 252 | 3 | 4.8 | 16,500 | 4.5 |
| 5'x8'x7' | 280 | 4 | 5.4 | 19,000 | 5 |
| 6'x8'x7' | 336 | 5 | 6.6 | 22,500 | 6 |
| 6'x9'x7' | 378 | 5 | 7.2 | 25,500 | 7 |
| 8'x8'x7' | 448 | 6 | 8.8 | 30,000 | 8 |
| 8'x10'x7' | 560 | 8 | 11.2 | 37,500 | 9 |

*Kiuas* units are available in rectangular, octagonal, round, or triangular (for corner installation) design, either to be set on the floor or hung from the wall.

# A Project for Do-It-Yourselfers
## The Bathhouse Itself

Steam baths of diverse kinds have been developed over the years. In his historic account of bathing practices, *Clean and Decent*, Lawrence Wright describes some of the ingenious designs: the 1756 British model, consisting of a wooden box with hole for the head and using steam provided by a kettle; the 1814 United States version of a boiler directing steam under bedclothes; the production in 1855 of a bag tightened around the neck and fed by a small boiler; the bucket for pouring water on a heated brick to produce steam below a bather who is seated and covered with cloths or towels; the cylindrical steambox with chair. These generally have been variations of the current steam cabinets or steam rooms, which have high humidity and relatively low temperatures.

The sauna, in contrast, is basically a room in which high heat and only moderate humidity are developed. Whereas the steam bath operates at a temperature of about 120° F (50° C) and humidity up to 100 percent, the sauna has temperatures of 175–205° F (80–95° C) and humidity of about 15 percent.

The essentials of a sauna are elemental: a simple, wooden structure, rocks that can be heated, hot and cold air, hot and cold water. The design throughout the years has remained simple. The structure can therefore be built by a person who has a modicum of carpentry skills, or it can be purchased prefabricated at modest cost. If one has hesitated to acquire a sauna because it seems so strange, no sweat: the basic design is quite simple.

The ideal sauna is a small building made of logs, set near a lakeshore, facing toward the sunset. However, a sauna can easily be included as part of the design of a house. In keeping with the sauna mystique, the style of the construction should be simple and rustic, rather than fancy, chrome-plated.

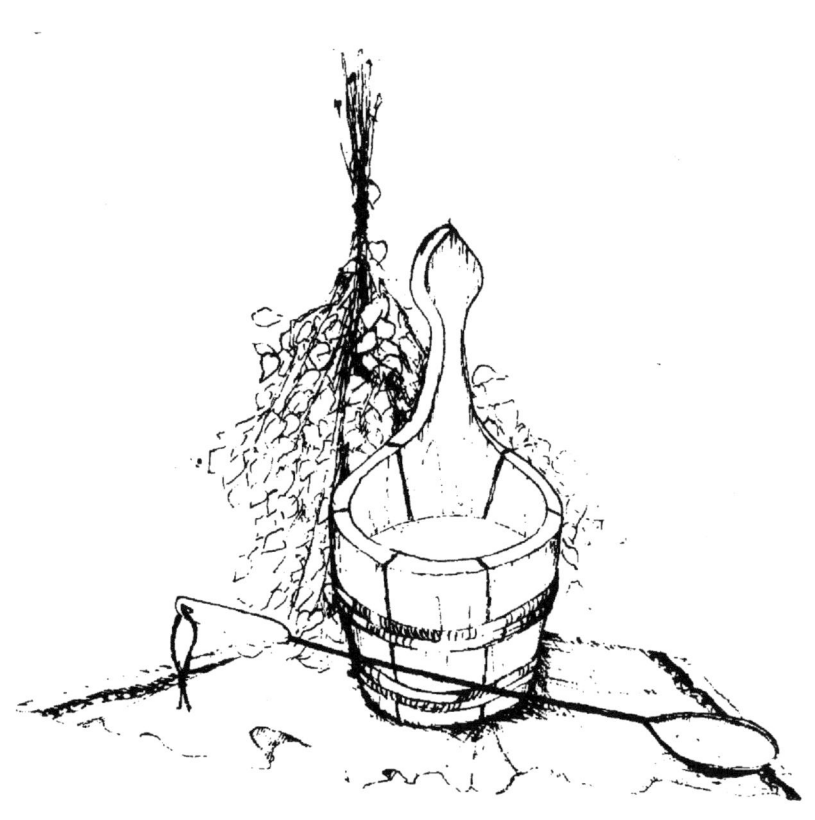

Sauna architecture, like all architecture, should be functional. "Form must follow function." The size of the sauna is determined by the number of bathers. The size of the heat room, particularly, is governed by the use for which it is intended: if two or four or eight people will regularly use the sauna at one time, there should be sufficient space for them on the *lauteet* or shelves.

A complete sauna will include three rooms: a heat room, a washing room, and a dressing room. When a sauna is constructed in a home, it is often sufficient to install only the heat room, since shower and dressing areas may be conveniently near. In any case, while washing may be done in the heat room, the preferred design has one room for steam-cleaning, another for washing. The French used to write "room of baths" *(salle de bains)* rather than "bathroom" because bathrooms in the time of Louis XV had two baths — one for washing, one for rinsing. We still follow that principle in our dishwashing — one section for washing, the other for rinsing — but in tub baths for people-washing, bathers remain in their dirtied wash water until they dry themselves.

The dressing room is simply a small room with places to sit and perhaps to lie down. The walls and ceiling need no special construction or materials.

The washroom usually includes shower facilities or water taps for washing from buckets. Any materials suitable for a shower may be used. In fact, a simple shower stall may be installed adjacent to the heat room.

The heat room is the unique unit in sauna construction. The interior walls, ceiling, and shelves should be of unpainted wood. This wood construction is an important factor in the sauna's uniqueness: the unpainted wood absorbs moisture and thus keeps humidity low, whereas non-porous materials like tile, cement, and painted or varnished surfaces would keep the moisture in the room — in the air or on the surfaces. Currently some manufacturers are promoting stainless steel, aluminum, and even fiberglass as easily cleaned and durable interior surfaces for saunas in commercial establishments, such as health clubs and motels. Those surfaces, however, destroy the authenticity of the sauna.

Several woods are well-suited for heat room construction. Redwood has been highly touted as an excellent choice. Impressed by its good moisture absorption, durability, resistance to warping, high insulation value, and striking beauty, many sauna manufacturers have used redwood for both interior and exterior paneling as well as for benches and duckboards. There is no doubt about it: redwood makes a fine sauna. Currently, however, two factors are causing a reassessment of redwood use: the comparatively high cost of the lumber and ecological concerns regarding the depletion of our nation's redwood stands. It seems inevitable that the predominance of redwood in the American sauna industry will decline, since several excellent, more moderately priced alternatives are available.

After all, in Finland, the home of the sauna, redwood is a little-used foreign import. Highly recommended woods for heating rooms are western red cedar, Engelmann spruce, sugar pine, cypress, aspen, and poplar. White cedar is fine for cedar chests and closets, but its odor is too strong for saunas. Clear-heart vertical-grain lumber is best, and in every case, the boards should be free of knots and pitch.

The construction style should be simple and practical. Laying the wallboards horizontally rather than standing them vertically is considered to give a more relaxed, restful setting. Door and window frames need not have mitered corners — simple butting, with the top piece slightly overlapping, gives a primitive beauty. Concern for singed fingers dictates wooden rather than metal door handles.

Sauna purists insist on a *savusauna*, a wood-fired "smoke sauna," which, instead of a chimney, has a smoke hole in the ceiling. Such a primitive sauna is permeated with the incense of wood smoke, blackened with soot, but utterly clean! Sauna connoisseurs who sigh for the smoke saunas and complain, "They don't make them like they used to," are kin to all who mourn the passing of stone-ground flour and handmade furniture. The nostalgia is legitimate, because some good things have almost disappeared and are no longer available except to a privileged few. Nevertheless, the modern saunas are excellent and available to all.

The heat room can be heated in any number of ways. (In third-century Alexandria, warring factions used hundreds of thousands of volumes from Ptolemy's library to heat the popular baths!) Most American saunas currently use gas or electricity, although lakeside saunas are generally wood-fired. Confronted by possible energy shortages, Americans can be expected to increase the use of wood and gas while correspondingly decreasing the use of electricity for sauna heating. If gas or electricity is used as the fuel, the proper line must be run to the *kiuas*. If electricity is used, a 220-volt line with No. 10 BX cable is required for all except the smallest units. If gas heating is chosen, proper venting must also be provided.

The *kiuas* is the heart of the sauna, consisting of a heating unit covered with stones. The stones generally range from the size of an egg to the size of a head of lettuce. Larger stones are placed at the bottom, smaller ones on top. Since these rocks are key to effective steam formation, they should be carefully selected. Only with superheated stones will the water vaporize explosively, immediately, and completely. To withstand heat of 700–1100° Fahrenheit, the stones should be hard, so that they will not crumble; round, to heat evenly and allow the hot air to circulate between them; without fissures, so cracks will not develop. Stones from a lakeshore, where they have withstood heat and cold, grinding and icing, often are good sauna stones. They can be further tested by hitting them with a hammer or by heating them red hot and dropping them into cold water. Stones that flunk either test should be thrown out. If the *kiuas* begins to heat more slowly, it should be checked for crumbling stones. In any case, the stones should be checked every two years. If they can't stand the heat they ought to get out of the *kiuas*. Recently promoted stoneless, metal grid heating stoves cannot compare with the stone-filled heaters.

The heating unit is encased in a masonry or metal housing. The heater should have sufficient capacity to heat the room adequately in an hour or an hour and a half. Although the sauna can be heated more quickly, a longer heating period gives the walls and ceiling time to "ripen" — to become thoroughly heated and super dry.

The tiered shelves on which bathers sit or lie are preferably made of aspen, which provides the coolest surface. Redwood, western cedar, and spruce are also popular. The surfaces should be finished with rounded edges and with no nail heads exposed. Sitting on the superheated nail heads can be very painful! The shelves are arranged against one or more walls. At least the top shelf should be long enough and wide enough for the bather to lie down. Quite often the top shelf is, in fact, a large platform. The bathing should take place higher than the *kiuas* top, where the real heat begins. Since most heating units are about two feet high, it is therefore customary to have two bathing shelves: one about 26 inches, the other about 38 inches from the floor. If the heating unit is hung on the wall, care should be taken that its top is not higher than the top shelf. A bench is usually placed in front of the first shelf to make a convenient step. This arrangement will leave a 40–46 inch distance from the top shelf to the ceiling. The total sauna height should be 75–84 inches. If washing or showering are to be included in the heat room, the ceiling height should be raised by a foot to provide less heat, more comfort at the washing level.

All parts of the sauna should be well ventilated but not drafty. In the heating room, where the average bather's oxygen consumption is 20 percent above normal, air should circulate freely to all parts of the room. The *kiuas* should not be solidly fenced in. Some have advocated boxing in the air beneath the shelves to cut down the air volume that must be heated. However, that area will unavoidably become damp and musty if enclosed. It is better to leave the space open and accessible for cleaning, thus helping provide a sufficient quantity of air for bathers. The heat room should not be airtight. The walls will breathe somewhat, of course. In addition, a space to allow air to enter should be provided under the door or by a louver set at the bottom of a wall, so that the oxygen supply will be sufficient. Moreover, an air outlet — window, louver, or exhaust fan — should be provided at the top of one of the walls facing the *kiuas* to ventilate the room properly after use.

A water line need not be run into the heat room. A bucket or two of water taken into the heat room will provide sufficient water for throwing on the rocks and for cooling the perspiring bathers. There should be a floor drain.

Lighting in the heat room should be subdued, producing an atmosphere of quiet. After all, it's light for relaxing, not reading. The light fixture installation is preferably on the wall rather than on the ceiling. The dressing room also should have quiet, non-glaring lighting. A window for natural light and a beautiful view of a lake would be ideal.

A sauna which is built as part of a house — at ground level, in the basement, upstairs, or even in the attic — should have the walls of the heat room insulated. Two-inch fiberglass insulation, with reflecting surface toward the inside of the room, can be placed between wall studs and between ceiling joists.

## Sauna Furnishings

To harmonize with the construction, sauna furnishings should be simple, natural, functional. It is advisable to have removable duckboards made of wooden slats on the floors of both the heat room and the shower room. Carpets of fiber mats are most appropriate for the floor of the dressing room.

Little equipment is needed in the heat room. A cup or wooden-handled dipper and wooden or plastic buckets are the only essentials. It should be remembered that, if wooden buckets are allowed to stand empty, the staves will dry out and shrink; the buckets should be kept full of water. In addition to the bare essentials, linen or terry cloth towels for the shelves are recommended. A wall thermometer and hygrometer are interesting additions, of course.

Basically, however, the room should be about as bare as the bathers. For the washing area, the normal shower accessories are appropriate: towel racks, soap and shampoo holders, soap and shampoo, plus possibly a bucket and stool for leisurely shampooing or foot soaking. There should also be some harsh scrubbing aids which, while removing dead skin and dirt, will also tone the skin and the muscles beneath. The Romans of old used a *strigil*, a curved metal scraper, in their hot baths. The current options are rough washcloths, stiff-bristled brushes, sponges (*luffas* — gourd sponges — are the favorites), or the ingenious sauna *piika*, a cloth scrubber of yarn which includes an abrasive nylon thread.

For the dressing area, the essential furnishings are benches, stools, or chairs; a small table; a mirror; a shelf for towels and grooming aids; and pegs or hooks for hanging clothes. The room is a place for drying, cooling off, sipping a refreshing drink, perhaps having a bite of something salty with the drink, and chatting with sauna partners while relaxed and refreshed. It is a place where lean, ascetic furnishings are appropriate: simple benches and rattan furniture, with natural finishes, rather than overstuffed discards from the living room or bulky cast-offs from the patio. Warm-hued carpets and textiles, simple glassware and ceramics — even colorful posters — fit in beautifully. Typically, seats are covered with towels. Beauty and grooming aids are often available. Sometimes a dressing room is equipped with refrigerator, dishes, and glassware, but cold drinks and snacks can easily be prepared in the kitchen and brought to the dressing room.

Sauna owners will often keep swimming suits, thongs, and wrap-around terry cloth beachwear in the dressing room for use after the bath — in a pool, on the patio, or for a backyard roll in the snow.

# A Variety of Designs

The homeowner who decides to acquire a sauna can accomplish that goal in a number of ways. He can simply contact a nearby sauna dealer and contract to have the sauna installed complete. Or he can decide to save some money by ordering the prefabricated components of a modular sauna and assembling them himself. Or he can order the still more economical package of pre-cut materials and construct the facility himself according to accompanying directions.

Noting the simplicity of sauna design, construction, and furnishings, the do-it-yourselfer can even opt to build a complete indoor or outdoor sauna himself, picking a suitable design, purchasing the heater from a sauna manufacturer, and buying the needed lumber from a local lumberyard. And, of course, there is always the option of obtaining a plan and hiring a carpenter to build the facility according to specifications. Drawings are readily available from suppliers and sauna consultants. Many options for saunas are offered on the Internet. Based on the growing popularity of saunas, sauna acquisition is more and more being considered an investment rather than an expenditure.

After opting for the joys of sauna ownership, one must answer the following questions:

1. Will it be an indoor or outdoor sauna? (The latter is a possibility in rural areas and at lakeside summer homes.)
2. Will it be a fully equipped sauna with heat room, shower room, and dressing room; or will it simply be a heat room, with other existing facilities used for showering and dressing?
3. Will it be a prefabricated sauna, one built specifically to the owner's needs, or an owner-built project?
4. What fuel will be used — wood, gas, or electricity?
5. What are the limits in cost?

Having decided precisely what is desired, one can locate suppliers by checking the yellow pages of the telephone directory under "Sauna Equipment and Supplies," "Hot Tubs and Spas," and "Wood Stoves."

Or search the Internet. Most sauna manufacturers have web pages. One also should use saunas at health clubs, Y's, motels, or private homes and ascertain how well satisfied the operators and users are with the units. Sauna heaters as well as complete prefabricated saunas have become readily available in all areas of our country. Suppliers are eager to provide brochures and price lists for various models. And sauna owners are usually proud to show their facilities to others.

# A Bridge Between Cultures

*by Maija Nelson*

Most Americans know little about Finland, the Nordic nation sandwiched between Russia on the east and Sweden on the west. Though Finland covers 130,000 square miles, the approximate area of Minnesota, the population measures in at only about five million.

This country is marked by its arctic chill and six-month winters in which the sun makes a brief appearance at midday. Such a climate calls for an opposite extreme, a wooden room steam-heated by ladles of water tossed over hissing, popping red stones. Sauna temperatures can reach over 200° Fahrenheit. Figuratively speaking, saunas might even be called ovens designed for human cooking!

Perhaps the most striking thing about this means for rejuvenation, this spot for relaxation, this aid to grooming is its all-inclusive nature. The sauna in Finland is frequented by persons of all ages. It serves as a means for socialization, for beautification, for relaxation, and for self-improvement; it is a place to encounter and interact with oneself and people of varied interests, to be equal in nudity and sensory consumption, to work on relationships and on oneself. For the people of my generation, the sauna is also a reason to gather socially. I experienced the sauna as a cultural routine and, therefore, part of my Finnish heritage, while studying in Finland during the second semester of my third year at Valparaiso University.

Saunas are everywhere! Most Finnish family homes include a sauna installed within a large shower room. Student apartments typically share one sauna per every four flats, with men's and women's open visitation hours and slots for individual reservations. Most Finns also own a summer cottage on a body of water; such a retreat is incomplete without both an indoor and outdoor sauna. A typical summer day spent at such a location may include sausage roasting, canoeing, swimming, and basking in a summer sun that turns the sky into brilliant warm colors and does not completely agree to set. Although

Finns enjoy outdoor sports and activities even throughout the six-month winter, they welcome the other six months that constitute summer, a lovely and energetic season.

For young adults like me, the sauna is multi-functional during all seasons. It provides a method of relaxation after a long day at school or a long day of skiing, a way to release the chill from one's bones after another day in the white outdoors, a place and time set aside each week for discussion and drinks with a friend or flat mate.

Saunas are a beauty or rejuvenation ritual shared with same-sex friends before a night out on the town, a cultural icon shared with family. The deep heat of a sauna can have either a relaxing or an invigorating effect; one leaves with either a desire for food and sleep or for company and dancing. Eventually most international student gatherings turn into sauna parties — perhaps the most facilitative kind for getting to know one another. Unlike the pretentious club or home party, people arrive to this sort of affair in their most comfortable attire. Rooms in an apartment-type sauna are segregated by sex, but there is always a common room with places to sit and food to eat where warm, comfortable bundles of young adults of all nationalities gather to share their ideas and to entertain one another. A little bit of Finnish non-pretense is a good starter for the kinds of relationships that one hopes will develop between young people with vastly different heritages, customs, and beliefs. By sharing in this Finnish ritual, they are expressing a general openness to cross-cultural adaptations. It's an ideal setting for the young and curious.

Another Finnish sauna tradition includes not only intense heat but also intense cold. It is a common practice in the wintertime to chip swimming holes out of the ice along the thousands of clear-water lakes and to circulate the water with pumps to inhibit the reformation of thick ice on the surface. After long bouts (up to twenty minutes or a half-hour) of skin-burning, blood-pumping subjection to steamy sauna heat, the bather runs straight down a rubber mat, off a short dock and immediately into heart-stopping ice water. This ritual may sound torturous to the unpracticed, but Finns testify to its effectiveness by boasting a healthy, fit population of elderly people. It has been explained that such an experience provides an effortless, though gutsy, cardiovascular workout and metabolic boost by forcing the body to adapt quickly to extreme differences in temperature. This practice is good not only for the heart and the lungs but also for the skin. Pores all over the body are opened by heat, flushed clean with sauna-induced sweat, then contracted quickly in the clean, icy water. This is highly beneficial to complexion. This practice is also advocated in many women's publications (i.e. *Cosmopolitan*) that advise readers to tolerate thirty seconds of chilly tap water following a steamy shower.

I was privileged to experience the sauna also as an occasion for sharing my heritage. During my winter stay in Finland I spent a number of vacation days with relatives living north of the Arctic Circle. Among the most memorable of my sauna experiences is one in which a third cousin invited me into her home, then made a bit of a ceremony of her newly built wood-burning summer sauna — an outdoor structure of two rooms, one the sauna and the other a small fireplace lounge. In the morning, I helped her start fires in the fireplace and oven; in the afternoon, we scooted enormous buckets of water on sleds from the house to the heat room. We lit many tiny candles in the changing room and placed them on the jutting rocks of the fireplace to create a meditative sort of environment in the evening with the sun down.

We drank cold homemade beer on the warm sauna benches until we were craving the cold. Then, in the dark, hiding our nakedness from the neighbors, we ran into the yard to roll in the snow, then returned to the sauna for more heat. We did this several times. Then we shampooed our hair and washed our bodies in the heat and rinsed ourselves with the stove water made tepid with armfuls of snow.

Although uniquely Finnish in origin, there are saunas and sauna fans all over the world. Those who have immersed themselves totally into the sauna experience agree that there's nothing quite like it for a physical, mental, and spiritual high.

# A Heated Competition

*by David Maki*

The Finnish sauna is typically a place to relax, to unwind, and to escape from the stressors of the day. However, for one weekend in Finland, the sauna becomes a place to prove your mettle, show off your *"sisu"* and "take the heat." Each year since 1999, the Sauna Bathing World Championships have taken place in August in Heinola, a city northeast of Helsinki in the Nordic country that has brought to the world such unusual competitions as the Wife Carrying Contest, the Mosquito Swatting Contest, and the Anthill Sitting Contest.

In the Sauna Bathing Championships, contestants battle one another in an effort to prove which one can physically tolerate the most heat and humidity for the longest time.

The sauna as a sporting event was unofficially started by a group of men whose Finnish machismo spilled over into their sauna. These informal competitions were quickly squashed when numerous sauna-enthusiasts — believing that they were about to relax and unwind — inadvertently walked into the "mist" of a competitive environment.

In the official championships, participants — wearing normal swimwear — must sit upright on the top bench, elbows on knees and arms in an upright position. Seats are determined by a lottery-style drawing. Organizers take care of the steam by pouring one-half liter of water on the 110° Celsius (nearly 230° Fahrenheit!) stove every 30 seconds. The winner is the last person remaining in the sauna — in the proper seated position. He or she must be able to exit the sauna under his or her own power.

In the inaugural championships of 1999, Finns emerged as both the male and female champions, with Ahti Merivirta and Katri Kamarainen coming out on top. Finland dominated the competition so greatly in 1999 that no other country's entrants managed to advance to the final round. The next year, salesman Leo Pusa took home the top spot from the men's competition, while Kamarainen repeated as the women's champion.

The event quickly grew into a major media spectacle. Television crews from Finland, France, and Germany come to Heinola each year, giving the unusual contest the feel of a major sporting event. Some 18,000 people — both residents and tourists — turned out to watch the finals in 2002, which featured eighty competitors from sixteen countries.

In 2001, Pusa again emerged as the top male sauna-goer, while border guard Annikki Peltonen earned top honors for the women. As an aside to the regular competition, Finland took on — and defeated — Sweden in a sauna-bathing match, claiming a 15-7 victory. In addition, everyone at the sauna championships also witnessed the first-ever wedding in a sauna, as a local couple tied the knot while the stove sizzled and the steam rose.

Pusa was the "top dog of the top bench" in the 2002 competition for the men; however, his 12-minute, 10-second stay in the steam was outdone by reigning women's champion Peltonen, who surpassed Pusa's effort by more than one minute in taking the women's crown. In fact, all three of the top female finishers surpassed the 13-minute mark, while Pusa was the lone male to achieve a stay of greater than 12 minutes.

The Sauna Bathing World Championships, born from a "heated" competition between friends in a public sauna, has evolved into an international spectacle.

God did not invent hurry.

*— A Finnish Proverb*
*from the book* Scandinavian Proverbs

# Sauna 101

*by Bernhard Hillila*

Here we're back to basics, the four elements
known by the ancients — earth, air, fire, water.

**Take earth —**
a clearing set near birch trees, if possible,
or part of an apartment complex on Maple St. will do.

**Take water —**
running in a stream nearby, or a lakeful, if possible,
or make do with a shower stall in the corner.

**Take air —**
light-night air of June and St. John's Eve, when possible,
or January air of stars and Northern Lights, when possible,
or even filtered April air in the Shreveport Holiday Inn.

**Take earth —**
transformed from red cedar cones to log walls,
from aspen seeds to platforms for bathers,
from birch seeds to whisks for switching skin.

**Take fire —**
a kerosene lamp, if possible, or an electric bulb will do.

**Take earth —**
mined as ore and forged into a cast iron stove;
into the stove load earth grown to trees, split to firewood;
at the top of the stove place earth —
glacier-hewn, frost-tested rocks found in the field
or sand-blasted, water-washed stones from the beach.

**Take fire —**
flame that wakens dormant heat; touch it to paper
made of pulp, flare it to kindling and logs, if possible;
or simply turn on the gas or the electric current;
then let fire work its magic, turning wood to smoke,
stones to warmth and air to blessing. (It's not
the humidity, it's the heat that makes a sauna.)

Take earth —
formed into earthlings, breathed to life with air,
touched by divine fire; insert them into the sauna
where the naked again can be innocent.

Take water —
throw it with a dipper formed from copper ore;
savor a heat cocktail of water-on-the-rocks —
become immersed in the warmth and relaxation,
know comradeship, sense healing and mystery.

Take air —
moved by *kiuas,* switches, lungs; breathe it
gently, not as heavy steam but light vapor;
process it in conversation, sighs of satisfaction.

Take water —
pouring from pores and salted with living,
cascading in capillaries below invigorated skin.

Take air —
give it in gasps in the lake or shower,
in cooling breeze outside on the bench.

Take water —
give it for washing with *loofa* gourds or brushes
(you are here to come clean); use it
for summer skinny-dipping, if possible,
or for winter snow-dipping, perhaps.
(Is there anything cleaner than a Finn fresh
from sauna making angels in pure white snow?)
Or even a brisk shower will do.

Take earth —
reincarnated as coffee beans, wheat and cardamom,
and with fire and water, brew coffee, bake *pulla.*
Or take barley and hops harvested from the earth,
brewed with water and fire, and drink refreshment.

Take air —
leaving sauna, say "Aah!" Thanks for the sauna,
where your forebears took their first breaths,
where they were washed after their last breaths,
to be returned clean to the earth. Say "Aah!"

.

# POSTSCRIPT

After reading what I have had to say about the sauna, you may think *The Sauna Is . . .* something I'm too steamed up about! Nevertheless, I'd like to leave one final thought with you: if genius is 10 percent inspiration and 90 percent perspiration, try thinking through your problems in a sauna!

— *Bernhard Hillila*